Pet Rescue

Stories by Julia Donaldson

Contents

The Greyhound

Jack and Ella live in the country.
Their mum runs a pet rescue centre.
Jack and Ella love helping their
mum look after the animals.

One Saturday, Usman came to the
pet rescue centre.

"Usman is staying with us today,"
said Mum. "His mum has to go
to work."

"You can help us look after the
animals," said Jack.

"No, thanks," said Usman.

"I need to train for Sports Day.
I want to win the running race."

Usman ran round the field.

"How fast was I?" he asked.

"You took five minutes," said Ella.

"That's too slow," said Usman.

So he ran off round the field again.

Suddenly, Usman stopped running.

"Hey! Come and look at this,"
he shouted.

Jack and Ella ran over to Usman.

They saw a thin, grey dog tied to
a tree.

"She's got a bad leg," said Jack.

"I'll run quickly and get your mum,"
said Usman.

Soon Usman came back with Mum.

Mum looked at the dog.

"This is a racing greyhound," she said.

"But she cannot race with a bad leg.

Maybe that's why her owner doesn't

want her anymore."

Usman, Jack and Ella helped
Mum get the greyhound back to
the rescue centre.
"I think her leg hurts a lot," said Ella.
"Poor dog," said Usman. "How could
someone just leave her?"

Ella showed Usman how to
bandage the bad leg.
Jack showed him how to brush
the dog's coat.
"She looks a lot better now,"
said Mum.
"Let's call her Flash," said Usman.
Flash gave Usman a lick.

Later on, Usman's mum came to collect him.

"Have you done lots of running today?" she asked.

"No," said Usman. "I've been looking after a dog. Come and see."

"This is Flash," said Usman.

"Her owner doesn't seem to want her anymore."

Usman gave Flash a hug.

"Can Flash come to live with us?" asked Usman. "I'd look after her."

"She's a lovely dog," said Usman's mum.

"Would you like us to look after Flash?" asked Usman's mum.

"That would be great," said Mum.

"When her leg is better, you can both go running," said Jack.

"Yes," said Usman. "Maybe she will help me win the running race."

Deep Danger

Jack and Ella were walking home
from school. They passed an
empty house.

"Can you hear that noise?" asked Jack.

"It sounds like someone crying,"
said Ella.

They looked into the garden.

"It's coming from that old well,"

said Ella.

"Come on," said Jack. "Let's take

a look."

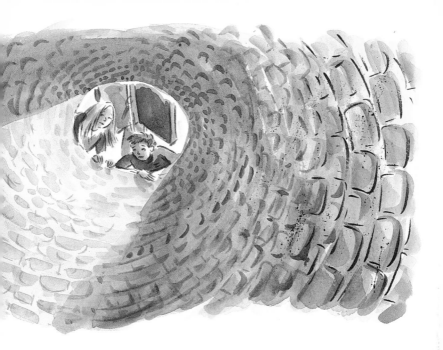

Jack and Ella went into the garden.

They looked down the old well.

They could see something moving at
the bottom.

"It's some kittens!" said Ella.

"We must get them out!" said Jack.

"No, it's too dangerous," said Ella.

"You go and get Mum. She'll know
what to do."

Then it began to rain.

"Oh no!" said Ella. "If the water in the well gets deeper, the kittens will drown."

Two of the kittens looked up at Ella.
The third kitten did not move.

Jack came running back with Mum.

"We've called the fire brigade,"
he said.

Just then the fire engine arrived.

Two firefighters got out.

They looked down the well.

"Poor little things," said one firefighter.

The firefighters put a ladder down into the well. One of them started to climb down. The rain was pouring down. The water in the well was getting deeper and deeper.

At last, the firefighter climbed back out. He was holding two very wet kittens. He handed them to Jack and Ella. Then he went back down into the well.

Soon the firefighter came back with the last kitten. He looked very sad.

The last kitten was dead.

Ella and Jack were very upset.

Mum gave them both a hug.

"How did the kittens get into the well?" asked Jack.

"Someone must have thrown them in," said Mum.

"But that's so cruel," said Ella.

"I know," said Mum. "But sometimes people don't want their pets.

You and Jack saved *two* of them."

"Come on," said Mum. "Let's get
these two back to the rescue centre.
We can help *them* to get better."
Mum, Jack and Ella carried the
kittens very gently back to the van.

Old Dog

Penny was a very old dog.
She was the oldest dog at the
pet rescue centre.

"I wish we could find her a home,"
said Ella.

"I don't think anyone will choose
Penny," said Mum. "She may have to
be put down."

Just then, Gemma arrived with her dad.

Gemma was one of Ella's friends.

"We've come to choose a dog,"
said Gemma.

Gemma and her dad looked at all the
dogs, but they couldn't find one that
was right for them.

"Why don't you have Penny?" said Ella.

"She's really friendly," said Jack.

"Penny is a lovely dog," said Gemma's dad, "but we want a young dog. We want to take it for lots of walks."

"There's a dog in our road that is never taken for walks," said Gemma. "It never stops barking."

"It drives us mad!" said her dad.

"Anyway, we'll be going now. None of these dogs are quite right for us."

After Gemma and her dad had gone
home, Mum said to Jack and Ella,
"I wonder why that dog barks so
much. He must be very unhappy.
I'm going to find out why."

Mum, Jack and Ella went to Gemma's road. They saw the dog tied up in a garden. It was barking loudly.

"He looks really bored," said Ella.

"Wait here," said Mum. "I'm going to talk to the owner."

Soon Mum came back with an
old man.

"This is Mr Penrose," said Mum.

"He wants us to find Bouncer a
new home."

"Yes," said Mr Penrose, sadly.

"Bouncer likes long walks and I'm
getting too old to take him out."

Mr Penrose gave Bouncer's lead to Mum.

He still looked very sad.

Then Jack had an idea.

"Come back to the rescue centre
with us, Mr Penrose," said Jack.

"I want to show you something."

At the rescue centre, Jack led

Mr Penrose to Penny.

Penny put her paw out to the old man.

"She seems a lovely dog," said

Mr Penrose.

"And she doesn't need to go for

long walks," said Jack.

"So maybe you could give Penny a home," said Ella.

"I think that's a grand idea," said Mr Penrose.

"And then Gemma could have Bouncer," said Jack.

Jack and Ella looked at Mum.

"Let's ring Gemma now," said Mum.